Germany Unveiled

A Traveler's Etiquette Guide to Germany

The Rover

Copyright © 2024 The Rover

INTRODUCTION

Welcome to Germany

Germany, renowned for its rich history, stunning landscapes, and vibrant culture, welcomes travelers from around the world with open arms. As you embark on your journey through this fascinating country, it's essential to embrace the cultural nuances and social norms that define German society.

Upon arrival, you'll be greeted by a diverse tapestry of experiences, from the bustling streets of Berlin to the serene beauty of the Bavarian countryside. Each region offers its own unique charm and character, waiting to be discovered and explored.

As you venture forth, remember to approach your interactions with curiosity, respect, and an open mind. Embrace the opportunity to engage with locals, immerse yourself in traditional customs, and savor the flavors of authentic German cuisine.

From the orderly efficiency of public transport to the convivial atmosphere of beer gardens and festivals, Germany offers a wealth of experiences for travelers of all interests. By observing local customs, practicing cultural sensitivity, and demonstrating courtesy and respect, you'll forge meaningful connections and create lasting memories during your time in Germany.

So, welcome to Germany, a land of history, culture, and hospitality. May your journey be filled with wonder, discovery, and the warmth of new experiences. Enjoy your travels, and immerse yourself in all that this remarkable country has to offer.

Importance of Cultural Awareness

Cultural awareness is a vital aspect of traveling responsibly and respectfully in Germany. As you explore this diverse and dynamic country, understanding and appreciating its cultural nuances will enrich your experience and foster positive interactions with locals.

By being culturally aware, you demonstrate respect for German traditions, customs, and social norms, enhancing your ability to connect authentically with the people and communities you encounter. It allows you to navigate social situations with confidence and sensitivity, minimizing the risk of unintentionally causing offense or misunderstanding.

Furthermore, cultural awareness fosters empathy and understanding, enabling you to view the world through the lens of others and embrace diverse perspectives. It encourages you to approach unfamiliar situations with curiosity and an open mind, fostering meaningful connections and enriching cross-cultural exchanges.

In Germany, cultural awareness extends beyond mere etiquette; it encompasses an appreciation for the country's history, art, cuisine, and language. By immersing yourself in the local culture, you gain a deeper understanding of Germany's identity and heritage, enhancing your overall travel experience.

Ultimately, cultural awareness serves as a bridge that connects travelers with the essence of a destination, allowing them to engage authentically with its people and traditions. Embracing cultural awareness is not only a sign of respect but also a pathway to meaningful and memorable travel experiences in Germany and beyond.

UNDERSTANDING GERMAN CULTURE

Cultural Values and Traditions

Germany is a country rich in cultural heritage, shaped by centuries of history, tradition, and innovation. Understanding the cultural values and traditions that underpin German society is essential for travelers seeking to navigate the country with respect and sensitivity.

One of the central tenets of German culture is punctuality and reliability. Germans place a high value on timeliness and expect others to adhere to schedules and appointments. Arriving late is considered disrespectful and may be perceived as a lack of consideration for others' time.

Another key aspect of German culture is the emphasis on orderliness and efficiency. Germans take pride in their well-organized systems and expect visitors to respect rules and regulations, whether it be on public transportation, in public spaces, or at cultural sites.

Moreover, Germans value directness and honesty in communication. They appreciate clear and straightforward communication, even if it may seem blunt or brusque to outsiders. Being honest and transparent in your interactions will be appreciated and respected.

Family and community are also important cultural values in Germany. Germans maintain close-knit relationships with family members and often prioritize spending time together. Additionally, community involvement and participation in local events and traditions are highly valued.

Traditions such as Oktoberfest, Christmas markets, and regional festivals play a significant role in German culture, offering opportunities for locals and visitors alike to come together and celebrate. Embracing these traditions can provide valuable insights into German life and foster connections with the local community.

Overall, by respecting cultural values such as punctuality, orderliness, honesty, and community, travelers can navigate German society with grace and appreciation, gaining a deeper understanding of the country's rich cultural tapestry.

Etiquette & Social Norms

Navigating social interactions in Germany requires an understanding of the country's etiquette and social norms, which play a significant role in daily life and interactions with others. By familiarizing yourself with these customs, you can ensure respectful and harmonious communication with locals.

One of the fundamental aspects of German etiquette is politeness and courtesy. Germans value polite behavior and expect visitors to greet others with a handshake and a verbal greeting, such as "Guten Tag" (Good day) or "Hallo" (Hello), particularly in formal settings. It's also customary to address people using their title and last name until given permission to use their first name.

Respecting personal space is another important aspect of German social norms. Germans tend to maintain a relatively large personal space and may feel uncomfortable with close physical proximity during conversations. It's essential to be mindful of personal boundaries and avoid invading others' personal space.

Directness and honesty are highly valued in German communication. Germans appreciate straightforwardness and expect others to express their opinions openly and honestly, even if it means delivering constructive criticism. Being diplomatic yet honest in your communication will be appreciated and respected.

When dining out or attending social gatherings, it's customary to wait until everyone is seated and the host offers a toast before beginning the meal. Additionally, it's polite to wait for the host to initiate conversations and to offer compliments on the food or ambiance.

Tipping is customary in Germany but is generally less generous than in some other countries. It's common to round up the bill to the nearest euro or add a 5-10% tip for good service. However, tipping is not mandatory, and it's acceptable to tip based on the level of service received.

Overall, by observing the principles of politeness, respecting personal space, communicating directly and honestly, and adhering to dining etiquette, travelers can navigate social interactions in Germany with confidence and respect for local customs and traditions.

SOCIAL INTERACTION

Greetings & Introductions

In Germany, greetings and introductions play an important role in establishing rapport and showing respect in social interactions. Understanding the appropriate ways to greet others and introduce yourself will help you navigate cultural norms with ease.

When meeting someone for the first time, a handshake is the most common form of greeting in Germany. A firm handshake accompanied by direct eye contact conveys confidence and respect. It's customary to address the person using their title and last name until given permission to use their first name.

The most common greeting in German is "Guten Tag," which translates to "Good day." This greeting is appropriate for formal and informal situations alike and can be used throughout the day. "Hallo" is a more casual greeting that can be used among friends or acquaintances.

When entering a room or joining a group conversation, it's polite to greet everyone individually with a handshake and a verbal greeting. Avoid simply nodding or waving from a distance, as this may be perceived as impolite or dismissive.

In more formal settings, such as business meetings or professional events, it's customary to greet others with a more formal tone and address them using their title and last name. For example, "Guten Morgen, Herr Schmidt" (Good morning, Mr. Schmidt) or "Guten Abend, Frau Müller" (Good evening, Mrs. Müller).

When introducing yourself, it's polite to state your full name and offer a brief handshake. For example, "Mein Name ist Anna Müller" (My name is Anna Müller). If you're meeting someone for the first time, it's also common to exchange pleasantries and ask about their well-being before diving into the conversation.

Overall, by mastering the art of greetings and introductions in Germany, you'll be able to navigate social interactions with grace and confidence, fostering positive connections with locals and creating memorable experiences during your travels.

Personal Space & Gestures

Respecting personal space is an essential aspect of German social etiquette. Germans tend to maintain a relatively large personal space and may feel uncomfortable with close physical proximity during interactions. Understanding and respecting these boundaries is crucial for smooth and respectful communication.

When engaging in conversations, it's important to maintain a comfortable distance from others, typically around an arm's length apart. Invading someone's personal space by standing too close may be perceived as intrusive or aggressive, so be mindful of giving others their space.

Germans also value nonverbal communication and may use subtle gestures to convey meaning or express themselves. For example, maintaining eye contact during conversations is considered a sign of attentiveness and respect. Avoiding eye contact may be interpreted as disinterest or insincerity.

Hand gestures are another aspect of nonverbal communication in Germany. While Germans tend to use fewer hand gestures compared to some other cultures, they may use subtle movements to emphasize points or convey emotion. However, excessive gesturing or flamboyant movements may be seen as exaggerated or insincere.

It's important to be aware of cultural differences in body language and gestures to avoid misunderstandings. For example, the "thumbs-up" gesture, commonly used in some countries to signal approval or agreement, may be interpreted differently in Germany and may even be considered offensive in certain contexts.

Overall, by respecting personal space, being mindful of nonverbal cues, and avoiding overly expressive gestures, travelers can navigate social interactions in Germany with grace and sensitivity, fostering positive connections and meaningful exchanges with locals.

Conversation Topics to Avoid

While Germans appreciate open and honest communication, there are certain topics that are best avoided in social settings to prevent discomfort or offense. Being mindful of these conversation topics will help you navigate social interactions with sensitivity and respect.

1. **World War II and the Holocaust:** Germany's history during World War II and the Holocaust is a sensitive subject that should be approached with caution. Avoid making casual references to these events or engaging in discussions that may evoke painful memories for Germans or individuals directly affected by these tragedies.

2. **Politics and Religion:** Discussions about politics and religion can be divisive and may lead to disagreements or tension. Unless you're in a formal setting where these topics are relevant, it's best to steer clear of controversial political or religious discussions.

3. **Personal Finances:** Inquiring about someone's salary or financial situation is considered intrusive in German culture. Personal finances are considered a private matter, and it's generally impolite to ask about someone's income or financial status.

4. **Personal Appearance and Weight:** Commenting on someone's physical appearance, weight, or personal grooming habits is considered inappropriate in Germany. Avoid making unsolicited remarks about someone's body or appearance, as it may be perceived as rude or intrusive.

5. **National Stereotypes:** Making generalized statements or jokes about Germans or other nationalities can be offensive and perpetuate stereotypes. Avoid making assumptions based on nationality and focus on engaging with individuals based on their unique personalities and experiences.

6. **Personal Health Issues:** Discussions about personal health issues or medical conditions are considered private matters in Germany. Avoid asking intrusive questions about someone's health or sharing details about your own health unless it's relevant to the conversation and the other person is comfortable discussing it.

By avoiding these sensitive topics and maintaining a respectful and considerate demeanor in social interactions, you'll be able to navigate conversations with ease and foster positive connections with locals during your travels in Germany.

DINING ETIQUETTE

Table Manners & Dining Customs

Dining in Germany is not just about enjoying delicious food; it's also an opportunity to experience the country's rich culinary traditions and social customs. Understanding German table manners and dining etiquette will help you navigate meals with grace and respect.

1. **Seating Arrangements:** In formal settings, the host may assign seating arrangements, with honored guests seated closest to the host. Wait for the host to indicate where you should sit before taking your seat.

2. **Use of Utensils:** Germans typically use both a fork and knife to eat most dishes. The fork is held in the left hand, and the knife in the right hand, with the cutting edge facing inward. After cutting food, place the knife on the edge of the plate with the blade facing inward.

3. **Bread and Bread Rolls:** Bread is a staple of German cuisine and is often served with meals. Tear off bite-sized pieces of bread rather than cutting it with a knife. It's customary to place a bread roll directly on the table rather than on a bread plate.

4. **Napkin Etiquette:** Place your napkin on your lap upon sitting down, and use it to dab your mouth as needed throughout the meal. At the end of the meal, place your napkin neatly on the table to the left of your plate.

5. **Ordering and Paying:** In restaurants, it's polite to wait for everyone at the table to be ready to order before calling the waiter over. When the bill arrives, it's common for each person to pay their share individually rather than splitting the bill evenly.

6. **Toasting:** Toasts are common during meals and celebrations in Germany. Raise your glass and make eye contact with the person you're toasting, saying "Prost!" (Cheers) before taking a sip. It's customary to maintain eye contact during the toast and to clink glasses with everyone at the table.

7. **Eating Pace:** Germans tend to eat at a leisurely pace, savoring each bite and engaging in conversation between bites. Avoid rushing through your meal or finishing before others at the table, as this may be considered impolite.

8. At the end of the meal, it's polite to express appreciation to the host or restaurant staff for the meal. A simple "Danke für das Essen" (Thank you for the meal) is a gracious way to show gratitude.

By observing these dining customs and table manners, you'll be able to enjoy meals in Germany with confidence and respect for local traditions. Embrace the opportunity to savor delicious cuisine while connecting with others over shared experiences and culinary delights.

Tipping Practices

Tipping in Germany is generally appreciated but less common and less generous than in some other countries. While tipping is not mandatory, it is customary to leave a small gratuity as a token of appreciation for good service. Here are some guidelines for tipping in Germany:

1. **Restaurants:** In restaurants, it's common to round up the bill to the nearest euro or leave a 5-10% tip for good service. However, tipping is discretionary, and you should base the amount on the level of service received. If you're paying by card, you can indicate the tip amount when entering your PIN or leave cash on the table when paying the bill.

2. **Cafes and Bars:** Tipping in cafes and bars is less common than in restaurants but still appreciated for exceptional service. You can round up the bill or leave a small tip if you're satisfied with the service, but it's not obligatory.

3. **Taxi Drivers:** Tipping taxi drivers is customary but not required. You can round up the fare to the nearest euro or add a small tip if the service was particularly good.

4. **Hotel Staff:** It's customary to tip hotel staff, such as bellhops or housekeeping, for their assistance and service. A small gratuity of 1-2 euros per bag for bellhops and a few euros per night for housekeeping is customary.

5. **Tour Guides and Drivers:** If you're on a guided tour or using the services of a private driver, it's customary to tip at the end of the service. A tip of 5-10% of the total cost of the tour or ride is generally appreciated for excellent service.

6. **Other Services:** Tipping for other services, such as hairdressers, spa treatments, or tour guides, is discretionary and depends on the level of service and your satisfaction. A tip of 5-10% is typically appropriate for exceptional service.

Remember that tipping practices may vary depending on the region and the establishment, so it's always a good idea to check if a service charge has already been included in the bill. Ultimately, tipping in Germany is a gesture of appreciation for good service, and any gratuity you choose to leave will be welcomed with gratitude.

Ordering & Paying at Restaurants

Navigating the dining experience at restaurants in Germany involves a few key etiquette considerations, from placing your order to settling the bill at the end of the meal. Here's what you need to know:

1. **Seating:** In many restaurants, you may choose your own seat unless a host directs you to a specific table. If you're unsure, it's polite to ask the staff for guidance.

2. **Menu Selection:** Take your time to peruse the menu before placing your order. When you're ready, signal to the waiter or waitress by making eye contact or raising your hand politely.

3. **Table Service:** In most restaurants, you'll receive table service, with the waiter or waitress taking your order, serving your food, and attending to any additional requests you may have. Be patient and courteous during the service.

4. **Special Requests:** If you have dietary restrictions or preferences, don't hesitate to inform your server when placing your order. They will do their best to accommodate your needs.

5. **Splitting Bills:** While it's common in some countries to split the bill evenly among diners, this practice is less common in Germany. Instead, each person typically pays for their own meal. If you're dining with a group, let the server know how you'd like the bill divided when requesting it.

6. **Paying the Bill:** When you're ready to pay, signal to the server by making eye contact or raising your hand discreetly. You can ask for the bill by saying "Die Rechnung, bitte" (The bill, please). Payment can be made in cash or by card, and it's customary to leave a small tip if you're satisfied with the service.

7. **Leaving the Restaurant:** After paying the bill, it's polite to thank the staff for their service before leaving the restaurant. A simple "Danke schön" (Thank you) or "Auf Wiedersehen" (Goodbye) is appreciated.

By following these guidelines for ordering and paying at restaurants in Germany, you'll be able to enjoy your dining experience with confidence and courtesy, while respecting local customs and etiquette.

PUBLIC BEHAVIOR

Public Transport Etiquette

Public transportation in Germany is known for its efficiency and reliability, and observing proper etiquette ensures a smooth and pleasant journey for everyone. Here are some key etiquette guidelines to keep in mind:

1. **Queueing:** When waiting for buses, trams, or trains, form a neat and orderly queue at the designated stops or platforms. Avoid crowding or pushing, and allow passengers to exit before boarding.

2. **Priority Seating:** Priority seating is reserved for elderly passengers, pregnant women, individuals with disabilities, and parents with young children. If you're seated in a priority area and someone in need boards the vehicle, offer your seat to them.

3. **Quiet Zones:** Some trains and trams have designated quiet zones where passengers are expected to refrain from talking loudly or using electronic devices. Respect these areas and keep noise to a minimum to ensure a peaceful environment for all passengers.

4. **Ticket Validation:** Always remember to validate your ticket before boarding public transportation. Failure to do so may result in a fine if caught by ticket inspectors.

Keep your ticket handy during your journey, as you may be asked to show it at any time.

5. **Boarding and Exiting:** Allow passengers to exit before boarding, and step to the side to make room for others. When exiting the vehicle, be mindful of your surroundings and watch for cyclists or pedestrians.

6. **Personal Space:** Respect the personal space of fellow passengers by avoiding intrusive behavior, such as leaning on them or placing belongings on adjacent seats. Keep backpacks and other bulky items out of the way to maximize space for everyone.

7. **Hygiene:** Maintain good personal hygiene while using public transportation, and be considerate of others by refraining from strong-smelling foods or perfumes. Dispose of any trash properly and leave the vehicle clean for the next passengers.

8. **Emergency Exits:** Familiarize yourself with the location of emergency exits and procedures in case of an emergency. Follow the instructions of the driver or conductor and remain calm to ensure everyone's safety.

By observing these etiquette guidelines, you'll contribute to a pleasant and respectful atmosphere on public transportation in Germany, enhancing the travel experience for yourself and your fellow passengers.

Queuing & Waiting in Line

Queuing and waiting in line are integral parts of daily life in Germany, and observing proper etiquette ensures fairness and orderliness in public spaces. Here's how to queue and wait in line respectfully:

1. **Forming a Queue:** When waiting in line for services, such as at ticket counters, grocery stores, or tourist attractions, join the end of the line and wait your turn. Avoid cutting in line or attempting to jump ahead, as this is considered rude and disrespectful.

2. **Maintaining Distance:** While waiting in line, maintain a respectful distance from the person in front of you to ensure personal space and comfort. Avoid standing too close or crowding others, as this can cause discomfort and tension.

3. **Patience and Courtesy:** Waiting in line may require patience, especially during busy times or in crowded spaces. Remain calm and courteous, refraining from pushing, shoving, or expressing frustration. Keep in mind that everyone is waiting their turn.

4. **Allowing Space:** If you're waiting in line in a confined space, such as on public transportation or in a crowded venue, be mindful of your surroundings and make space for others to pass by if needed. Step to the side to allow people to exit or enter without obstruction.

5. **Priority Queuing:** In some situations, such as at train or bus stops, priority queuing may be in place for certain passengers, such as elderly individuals, pregnant women, or individuals with disabilities. Respect these priority queues and allow those in need to board first.

6. **Queue Management:** If you're in a situation where there is no clearly defined queue, such as at a crowded event or attraction, be mindful of others and maintain order by forming a single-file line. Follow the lead of those around you and wait patiently for your turn.

7. **Exiting the Queue:** If you need to leave the queue for any reason, such as to use the restroom or retrieve something, inform those around you and step out of line politely. When you return, rejoin the queue at the appropriate place.

By adhering to these guidelines for queuing and waiting in line, you'll contribute to a respectful and orderly environment in public spaces, fostering a positive experience for yourself and those around you.

Smoking Regulations

Smoking regulations in Germany have evolved in recent years to reflect changing attitudes towards tobacco use and public health concerns. Here's what travelers need to know about smoking etiquette and regulations in Germany:

1. **Indoor Smoking Bans:** In Germany, smoking indoors is generally prohibited in public buildings, including restaurants, bars, cafes, and public transportation hubs. Many establishments have designated smoking areas or outdoor smoking areas where smokers can indulge.

2. **Designated Smoking Areas:** If you're a smoker, be mindful of designated smoking areas and adhere to local regulations. Look for designated smoking zones marked with signs or designated smoking rooms in hotels or airports where smoking is permitted.

3. **Outdoor Smoking:** Smoking is generally allowed in outdoor spaces, such as parks, sidewalks, and outdoor seating areas of restaurants or cafes. However, be considerate of others and avoid smoking in crowded or enclosed outdoor spaces where your smoke may affect non-smokers nearby.

4. **Respect Non-Smoking Areas:** Be mindful of non-smoking areas and respect the preferences of non-smokers. If you're in a public space or shared accommodation where smoking is prohibited, refrain from smoking or seek out designated smoking areas.

5. **Public Transportation:** Smoking is strictly prohibited on most forms of public transportation in Germany, including trains, buses, trams, and subway systems. Look for designated smoking areas at train stations or

outdoor platforms if you need to smoke while waiting for your train.

6. **Hotel Policies:** When staying in hotels or accommodations, familiarize yourself with the property's smoking policies. Many hotels offer both smoking and non-smoking rooms, so be sure to request a non-smoking room if you prefer.

7. **Dispose of Cigarette Butts Properly:** If you do smoke outdoors, be responsible and dispose of your cigarette butts properly in designated ashtrays or trash bins. Avoid littering or leaving cigarette butts on the ground, as this contributes to environmental pollution.

8. **Be Respectful:** Above all, be respectful of those around you, whether they smoke or not. Smoking is a personal choice, but it's important to be considerate of others' preferences and avoid imposing your smoke on non-smokers.

By understanding and adhering to smoking regulations and etiquette in Germany, you'll ensure a pleasant and respectful experience for yourself and those around you, while also promoting public health and environmental stewardship.

DRESS CODE & APPEARANCE

Dressing Appropriately for Different Occasions

Dressing appropriately for various occasions is essential to blend in with German society and show respect for cultural norms. Here's a guide to dressing appropriately for different situations in Germany:

1. **Formal Events:** For formal events such as business meetings, conferences, or upscale dinners, opt for conservative and professional attire. Men should wear a suit and tie, while women can choose a tailored dress, pantsuit, or skirt suit. Neutral colors and classic styles are typically preferred.

2. **Casual Outings:** Casual attire is suitable for everyday activities such as sightseeing, shopping, or dining at casual restaurants. Germans tend to dress casually but neatly, so opt for clean and comfortable clothing such as jeans, T-shirts, or casual dresses. Layers are also practical, especially in unpredictable weather.

3. **Cultural or Religious Sites:** When visiting cultural or religious sites, it's important to dress modestly out of respect for the place and its customs. Avoid wearing revealing clothing or items with offensive slogans or symbols. If necessary, bring a shawl or scarf to cover your shoulders or legs.

4. **Outdoor Activities:** Germany offers abundant opportunities for outdoor activities such as hiking, biking, or exploring nature. Dress in layers and wear sturdy footwear suitable for walking or hiking. Don't forget to bring a waterproof jacket or umbrella, as the weather can be unpredictable, especially in mountainous regions.

5. **Dining Out:** While casual attire is generally acceptable at most restaurants, it's a good idea to dress slightly more formally for upscale dining establishments. Men may opt for a collared shirt and trousers, while women can choose a nice blouse or dress. Avoid wearing overly casual or beachwear attire.

6. **Special Events:** For special events such as weddings, concerts, or theater performances, check the dress code specified on the invitation. Formal events may require dressier attire, such as cocktail dresses or suits, while more casual events allow for a wider range of clothing options.

7. **Seasonal Considerations:** Consider the season and weather conditions when choosing your attire. Germany

experiences distinct seasons, with warm summers and cold winters. In summer, lightweight clothing and sunscreen are essential, while in winter, dress warmly with layers, a coat, hat, and gloves.

8. **Footwear:** Comfortable and practical footwear is key for exploring Germany's cities and countryside. Opt for supportive shoes suitable for walking long distances, especially if you plan to sightsee or explore on foot. Avoid wearing flip-flops or sandals on city streets, as they may not provide adequate support.

By dressing appropriately for different occasions in Germany, you'll not only show respect for local customs but also ensure comfort and enjoyment during your travels. Remember to consider the specific dress codes and cultural expectations of each situation to make a positive impression and blend in seamlessly with German society.

Respect for Cultural & Religious Practices

Respecting cultural and religious practices is essential when visiting Germany to ensure harmonious interactions and demonstrate sensitivity to local customs. Here are some key considerations for respecting cultural and religious practices in Germany:

1. **Religious Sites:** When visiting churches, cathedrals, mosques, synagogues, or other religious sites, dress modestly out of respect for the sacredness of the space. Avoid wearing revealing clothing, hats, or sunglasses indoors, and adhere to any specific dress codes or guidelines posted at the entrance.

2. **Religious Holidays:** Germany celebrates a variety of religious holidays, including Christmas, Easter, and various Christian feast days. Respect these holidays by familiarizing yourself with local customs and traditions, such as attending church services, participating in festive events, or observing quiet periods of reflection.

3. **Public Displays of Affection:** Public displays of affection, such as kissing or hugging, are generally considered private matters in German culture. While it's acceptable to show affection to loved ones, particularly in casual settings, be mindful of the cultural norms and avoid overly affectionate behavior in public spaces.

4. **Cultural Sensitivity:** Germany is home to a diverse population, including people from various cultural and ethnic backgrounds. Show respect for cultural diversity by avoiding stereotypes or making assumptions based on appearance or ethnicity. Engage with people from different backgrounds with an open mind and curiosity, and be willing to learn about their traditions and customs.

5. **Language Use:** German is the official language of Germany, but many people also speak English, especially in tourist areas and major cities. While it's not necessary to be fluent in German, making an effort to learn basic phrases and greetings can demonstrate respect for the local language and culture. Use polite language and address people respectfully, especially elders or those in positions of authority.

6. **Cultural Heritage:** Germany has a rich cultural heritage, including art, music, literature, and architecture. Show appreciation for Germany's cultural contributions by visiting museums, attending concerts or theater performances, and exploring historical sites and landmarks. Respect the cultural significance of these treasures and follow any rules or guidelines for visitors.

7. **Environmental Stewardship:** Germans place a high value on environmental conservation and sustainability. Show respect for the environment by using public transportation, recycling and disposing of waste properly, and minimizing your carbon footprint during your stay. Respect local wildlife and natural habitats when exploring outdoor areas.

8. **Interfaith Dialogue:** Germany is home to a diverse array of religious communities, including Christian, Muslim, Jewish, and others. Foster interfaith dialogue and understanding by engaging respectfully with people of different faiths, learning about their beliefs and

practices, and participating in interfaith events or discussions.

By demonstrating respect for cultural and religious practices in Germany, you'll not only enhance your travel experience but also contribute to positive cross-cultural interactions and foster mutual understanding and respect among diverse communities.

RESPECT FOR THE ENVIRONMENT

Recycling & Waste Management

Germany is renowned for its commitment to environmental sustainability and efficient waste management practices. As a traveler, it's essential to familiarize yourself with recycling and waste management guidelines to minimize your environmental impact and adhere to local norms. Here's what you need to know:

1. **Separation of Waste:** In Germany, waste separation is taken seriously, with designated bins for different types of waste. Common categories include paper, plastics, glass, organic waste (compost), and general waste. Be sure to sort your waste correctly and dispose of it in the appropriate bins.

2. **Recycling Symbols:** Look for recycling symbols on packaging to determine how to dispose of items properly. Common symbols include the Green Dot (Grüner Punkt) for packaging recycling and the Mobius loop for recyclable materials. Familiarize yourself with these symbols to make informed decisions about waste disposal.

3. **Bottle Deposit System:** Germany operates a bottle deposit system (Pfand) for certain beverage containers, including glass and plastic bottles and aluminum cans. When purchasing beverages, you'll often pay a small deposit fee, which you can redeem by returning the empty containers to designated collection points, such as supermarkets or recycling centers.

4. **Reusable Bags:** Germany has taken steps to reduce plastic waste by implementing a ban on single-use plastic bags in many retail outlets. Bring reusable bags or backpacks for shopping, and consider using reusable containers for takeaway food or beverages to minimize packaging waste.

5. **Composting:** Many households in Germany participate in composting programs to recycle organic waste, such as food scraps and yard trimmings. If you're staying in accommodations with compost bins, be sure to separate organic waste from other waste streams and dispose of it accordingly.

6. **Hazardous Waste:** Certain items, such as batteries, electronics, and household chemicals, are considered hazardous waste and should not be disposed of in regular trash bins. Look for special collection points or recycling centers where you can safely dispose of these items.

7. **Public Recycling Facilities:** In addition to household recycling, Germany offers public recycling facilities and

collection points for items such as electronics, clothing, and bulky waste. Check local listings or inquire with your accommodation for information on nearby recycling centers.

8. **Reduce and Reuse:** Whenever possible, aim to reduce waste by choosing products with minimal packaging, opting for durable or reusable items, and repairing or repurposing items instead of discarding them. By embracing a "reduce, reuse, recycle" mentality, you can minimize your environmental footprint and contribute to a more sustainable future.

By adhering to recycling and waste management practices in Germany, you'll not only align with local environmental initiatives but also demonstrate respect for the country's commitment to sustainability. Play your part in preserving the environment for future generations and enjoy a more eco-conscious travel experience.

Outdoor Behavior & Nature Conservation

Germany boasts stunning natural landscapes, from lush forests and rolling hills to picturesque lakes and rivers. As a traveler, it's important to respect the environment and adhere to the principles of nature conservation. Here are some guidelines for outdoor behavior in Germany:

1. **Stay on Designated Paths:** When hiking or exploring nature trails, stick to designated paths to minimize your impact on the environment. Avoid trampling vegetation or disturbing wildlife habitats by straying off-trail.

2. **Leave No Trace:** Practice "Leave No Trace" principles by packing out all trash and waste, including food wrappers, bottles, and cigarette butts. Dispose of waste properly in designated bins or take it with you until you can dispose of it responsibly.

3. **Respect Wildlife:** Observe wildlife from a distance and avoid approaching or feeding animals. Keep noise levels to a minimum to avoid disturbing wildlife habitats and nesting areas. Respect any signs or barriers indicating protected or sensitive areas.

4. **Camp Responsibly:** If camping or picnicking in natural areas, choose established campsites and picnic areas whenever possible. Use designated fire pits or grills for cooking and never leave fires unattended. Respect quiet hours and minimize noise to preserve the tranquility of the surroundings.

5. **Protect Water Sources:** Keep water sources clean and free from contamination by avoiding washing dishes or bathing in streams or lakes. Use biodegradable soap if necessary and dispose of wastewater away from water sources.

6. **Respect Private Property:** Be mindful of private property boundaries and avoid trespassing on private land without permission. Stick to public trails and access points to avoid conflicts with landowners.

7. **Minimize Your Footprint:** Practice "leave only footprints" by minimizing your impact on the environment. Avoid picking flowers or disturbing natural features, and leave natural objects and artifacts undisturbed for others to enjoy.

8. **Educate Yourself:** Learn about local conservation initiatives, wildlife habitats, and environmental challenges in the areas you visit. Educate yourself about endangered species and conservation efforts to better appreciate and protect the natural beauty of Germany.

9. **Support Conservation Efforts:** Consider supporting local conservation organizations or participating in volunteer programs focused on environmental stewardship. Your contributions can help preserve and protect Germany's natural heritage for future generations to enjoy.

By following these guidelines for outdoor behavior and nature conservation in Germany, you'll not only enjoy a more enriching travel experience but also contribute to the preservation of the country's natural treasures. Respect for the environment is key to sustainable tourism and ensuring that Germany's natural beauty remains for generations to come.

CULTURAL SITES & RELIGIOUS ETIQUETTE

Visiting Churches, Temples, & Historic Sites

Germany is home to a rich cultural and religious heritage, with churches, temples, and historic sites that showcase centuries of history and architectural splendor. When visiting these sacred and significant places, it's essential to observe proper etiquette and show respect for the culture and traditions. Here are some guidelines to follow:

1. **Dress Modestly:** When visiting churches, temples, or other religious sites, dress modestly out of respect for the sacredness of the space. Avoid wearing revealing clothing, shorts, or sleeveless tops, and remove hats or sunglasses indoors.

2. **Quiet Reflection:** Maintain a quiet and respectful demeanor while inside religious buildings, refraining from loud conversation or disruptive behavior. Remember that these spaces are places of worship and contemplation for many people.

3. **Photography Restrictions:** Some churches, temples, and historic sites may have restrictions on photography or filming. Respect any signs or guidelines regarding photography and refrain from taking photos in prohibited areas or during religious ceremonies.

4. **Respectful Behavior:** Be mindful of your actions and avoid behaviors that may be considered disrespectful or offensive, such as touching religious artifacts or decorations, sitting or leaning on altars or religious symbols, or making loud noises.

5. **Follow Guided Tours:** If participating in a guided tour of a historic site or religious building, listen attentively to the guide's instructions and follow any rules or guidelines provided. Ask questions respectfully and refrain from disrupting the tour for other participants.

6. **Remove Footwear:** In some religious sites, it may be customary to remove your shoes before entering. Pay attention to any signs or instructions regarding footwear and follow the lead of other visitors or worshippers.

7. **Respect Religious Practices:** If visiting during a religious service or ceremony, observe quietly from the sidelines without interrupting or participating unless invited to do so. Be respectful of worshippers' religious practices and customs.

8. **Leave No Trace:** Practice "Leave No Trace" principles by refraining from littering, touching or

damaging historical artifacts or structures, or engaging in any behavior that may harm the environment or cultural heritage.

9. **Learn and Appreciate:** Take the time to learn about the history, significance, and cultural importance of the churches, temples, and historic sites you visit. Appreciate the craftsmanship, architecture, and spiritual significance of these places.

By following these etiquette guidelines when visiting churches, temples, and historic sites in Germany, you'll show respect for the culture and traditions while enjoying a meaningful and enriching travel experience. Remember to approach these sites with reverence and appreciation for their historical and cultural significance.

Dress Code & Behavior in Religious Spaces

When visiting religious spaces in Germany, it's important to adhere to certain dress codes and behaviors to show respect for the sacredness of these places and the beliefs of worshippers. Here are some etiquette guidelines to follow:

Dress Modestly: Dress modestly and conservatively when visiting churches, mosques, synagogues, or other religious sites. Avoid clothing that is too revealing, such as shorts, tank tops, or low-cut tops. Women may want to wear skirts or dresses that cover the knees, and men should avoid wearing hats indoors.

Remove Hats and Sunglasses: Remove hats, caps, or sunglasses before entering religious buildings, as wearing head coverings can be seen as disrespectful in some faiths. If you're unsure, observe the behavior of others or ask a local for guidance.

Covering Shoulders and Legs: In some religious spaces, particularly churches and mosques, it may be customary to cover your shoulders and legs. Carry a scarf or shawl to drape over your shoulders or wrap around your waist if you're needed. Respect any signs or guidelines regarding dress code posted at the entrance.

Maintain Quietness: Maintain a quiet and respectful demeanor while inside religious spaces, refraining from loud conversation, laughter, or disruptive behavior. Remember that these places are places of worship and reflection for many people.

Follow Guided Tours: If participating in a guided tour of a religious site, listen attentively to the guide's instructions and follow any rules or guidelines provided. Ask questions respectfully and avoid interrupting or disrupting the tour for other participants.

Respect Religious Practices: If visiting during a religious service or ceremony, observe quietly from the sidelines without interrupting or participating unless invited to do so. Be respectful of worshippers' religious practices and customs.

Be Mindful of Photography: Some religious sites may have restrictions on photography or filming, especially during religious services or ceremonies. Respect any signs or guidelines regarding photography and refrain from taking photos in prohibited areas.

Be Open to Learning: Take the opportunity to learn about the history, significance, and cultural practices of the religious space you're visiting. Respect the beliefs and traditions of worshippers and approach the experience with an open mind and heart.

By following these etiquette guidelines for dress code and behavior in religious spaces in Germany, you'll show respect for the sacredness of these places and create a more meaningful and respectful experience for yourself and others. Remember to approach religious sites with reverence and humility, regardless of your own beliefs.

ALCOHOL & DRINK CULTURE

Responsible Drinking & Socializing

Germany is known for its vibrant beer culture and lively social scene, but it's important to approach drinking and socializing responsibly to ensure a safe and enjoyable experience. Here are some etiquette guidelines to follow:

1. **Know Your Limits:** Pace yourself when drinking alcohol and know your limits. German beer can be stronger than what you're used to, so be mindful of how much you consume and avoid excessive drinking.

2. **Eat While Drinking:** Drinking on an empty stomach can lead to faster intoxication. Enjoy traditional German snacks such as pretzels, sausages, or cheese while drinking to help absorb alcohol and prevent overindulgence.

3. **Respect Local Customs:** Familiarize yourself with local drinking customs and traditions. In Germany, it's common to make eye contact and say "Prost!" (cheers)

before taking a sip of your drink. Wait for everyone to be served before clinking glasses and making a toast.

4. **Designated Driver:** If you're driving or using public transportation, plan ahead and designate a driver or arrange for alternative transportation options. Don't drink and drive, as it's illegal and dangerous.

5. **Watch Your Behavior:** Drinking can lower inhibitions, but it's important to maintain control and behave respectfully. Avoid loud or disruptive behavior, especially in public places or late at night, and be mindful of your language and actions.

6. **Respect Others' Limits:** Be respectful of others' choices regarding alcohol consumption. Don't pressure anyone to drink more than they're comfortable with, and be understanding if someone chooses not to drink at all.

7. **Stay Hydrated:** Alternate alcoholic drinks with water to stay hydrated and pace yourself throughout the evening. Drinking plenty of water can help prevent dehydration and lessen the effects of a hangover.

8. **Know Emergency Numbers:** Familiarize yourself with emergency numbers and services in case of any alcohol-related incidents or emergencies. Don't hesitate to seek help if you or someone else needs assistance.

9. **Enjoy Responsibly:** Above all, remember to enjoy yourself responsibly. Drinking can be a fun and social

activity, but it's important to prioritize your safety and well-being. Know when it's time to stop drinking and make arrangements to get home safely.

By practicing responsible drinking and socializing in Germany, you'll not only avoid potential health risks and legal issues but also ensure a more enjoyable and memorable experience. Cheers to responsible enjoyment and making lasting memories in the vibrant social scene of Germany.

Legal Drinking Age & Consumption Guidelines

Understanding the legal drinking age and consumption guidelines is essential when enjoying alcohol in Germany. Here's what you need to know:

1. **Legal Drinking Age:** The legal drinking age in Germany is 16 for beer and wine, and 18 for spirits (hard liquor). Minors under the age of 16 are generally not allowed to purchase or consume alcohol in public places, although exceptions may be made for supervised consumption at home or in certain cultural or religious contexts.

2. **Identification:** If you appear to be under the age of 25, you may be asked to show identification when purchasing alcohol. Carry a valid form of ID, such as a

passport or driver's license, to prove your age when necessary.

3. **Responsible Consumption:** While the legal drinking age may be lower than in some other countries, it's important to consume alcohol responsibly and in moderation. Know your limits and pace yourself when drinking, and be aware of the alcohol content of the beverages you're consuming.

4. **Public Drinking:** Drinking alcohol in public places is generally legal in Germany, although local regulations may vary. It's common to see people enjoying a beer in parks, at outdoor festivals, or along the riverside. However, always be respectful of others and avoid excessive public intoxication.

5. **Drinking and Driving:** Germany has strict laws against drinking and driving. The legal blood alcohol limit for drivers is 0.05%, and penalties for driving under the influence can be severe, including fines, license suspension, and even imprisonment. If you plan to drink, arrange for alternative transportation or designate a sober driver.

6. **Cultural Norms:** Drinking alcohol is deeply ingrained in German culture, with beer being a central part of the country's culinary heritage. However, excessive drinking or drunken behavior is generally frowned upon, especially in formal or business settings. Exercise

moderation and be mindful of your surroundings when consuming alcohol.

7. **Respect Local Customs:** When drinking with locals, follow their lead and observe local customs and traditions. Toasting (prost) is a common practice in Germany, and it's customary to make eye contact and clink glasses before taking a sip. Respect others' preferences regarding alcohol consumption and never pressure anyone to drink more than they're comfortable with.

By understanding and adhering to legal drinking age and consumption guidelines in Germany, you'll ensure a safe and enjoyable experience while partaking in the country's rich beer culture and social traditions. Drink responsibly and savor the unique flavors and traditions of German beverages.

Laws & Regulations in Germany

Understanding and respecting the laws and regulations in Germany is essential for travelers to ensure a smooth and enjoyable experience. Here's what you need to know:

1. **Legal Drinking Age:** The legal drinking age in Germany is 16 for beer and wine, and 18 for spirits (hard liquor). Minors under 16 are generally not allowed to purchase or consume alcohol in public places.

2. **Smoking Regulations:** Germany has strict regulations regarding smoking in public places. Smoking is prohibited in most indoor spaces, including restaurants, bars, and public transportation. Look for designated smoking areas or outdoor spaces where smoking is permitted.

3. **Traffic Laws:** Germany has stringent traffic laws, including speed limits, seatbelt requirements, and rules regarding mobile phone use while driving. Familiarize yourself with local traffic regulations and signage, and adhere to speed limits and traffic signals.

4. **Drinking and Driving:** Germany has zero tolerance for drinking and driving. The legal blood alcohol limit for drivers is 0.05%, and penalties for driving under the influence can be severe, including fines, license suspension, and imprisonment.

5. **Public Behavior:** Public drunkenness and disorderly conduct are not tolerated in Germany. Respectful behavior is expected in public spaces, including parks, streets, and public transportation. Avoid loud or disruptive behavior, especially late at night.

6. **Respect for Cultural Heritage:** Germany has a rich cultural heritage, and laws are in place to protect historical sites, monuments, and natural landscapes. Respect any signs or barriers indicating protected areas,

and avoid damaging or defacing cultural or natural landmarks.

7. **Environmental Conservation:** Germany is committed to environmental conservation and sustainability. Follow recycling and waste management guidelines, minimize your carbon footprint, and respect natural habitats and wildlife when exploring outdoor areas.

8. **Drug Laws:** Germany has strict laws regarding the possession and use of illegal drugs. Possession of even small quantities of illegal substances can result in severe penalties, including fines and imprisonment. It is illegal to use drugs in public places.

9. **Respect for Others:** Respect for others' rights, privacy, and personal space is paramount in Germany. Avoid intrusive behavior, refrain from taking photos of people without their consent, and be mindful of cultural sensitivities and social norms.

By familiarizing yourself with and adhering to the laws and regulations in Germany, you'll not only ensure your own safety and well-being but also demonstrate respect for the country and its people. Enjoy your time in Germany while staying informed and compliant with local laws.

Emergency Numbers & Services

Knowing the emergency numbers and services in Germany is crucial for travelers to ensure prompt assistance in case of emergencies. Here's what you need to know:

1. **Emergency Number:** The primary emergency number in Germany is 112. This number can be dialed for medical emergencies, fire, or police assistance anywhere in the country. It operates 24/7 and is free of charge.

2. **Police:** In non-emergency situations requiring police assistance, you can contact the local police station directly. The non-emergency police number is 110. Use this number for reporting crimes, filing complaints, or seeking general assistance from law enforcement.

3. **Medical Assistance:** For medical emergencies requiring ambulance services or medical assistance, dial 112. Trained operators will dispatch an ambulance to your location promptly. Be prepared to provide details about the nature of the emergency and your location.

4. **Fire Department:** In case of fires or other emergencies requiring fire department assistance, dial 112. The fire department will respond to fire-related incidents, rescue operations, and hazardous material spills.

5. **Language Assistance:** If you require language assistance when contacting emergency services, some operators may speak English or other languages. However, it's advisable to learn basic German phrases for emergency situations or have a translation app available on your phone.

6. **Consular Assistance:** If you're a foreign national and require assistance from your embassy or consulate, contact the nearest diplomatic mission. Embassy contact information, including emergency contact numbers, can typically be found on their official website.

7. **Insurance Coverage:** Before traveling to Germany, ensure that you have adequate travel insurance coverage, including medical and emergency evacuation coverage. Familiarize yourself with the terms and contact information for your insurance provider in case of emergencies.

8. **Keep Important Documents:** Keep copies of important documents, such as your passport, travel insurance policy, and emergency contact numbers, in a secure location separate from your original documents. This will facilitate assistance in case of loss or theft.

9. **Stay Calm and Communicate Clearly:** In case of emergencies, stay calm and provide clear and concise information to emergency operators. Follow their

instructions and cooperate with emergency responders to ensure a swift and effective response.

By familiarizing yourself with emergency numbers and services in Germany and taking proactive measures to prepare for potential emergencies, you'll be better equipped to handle unexpected situations and ensure your safety while traveling in the country.

CONCLUSION

Embracing German Culture with Respect & Courtesy

Germany boasts a rich and diverse cultural heritage, and travelers can enhance their experience by embracing German culture with respect and courtesy. Here are some insightful tips:

1. **Learn the Language:** While many Germans speak English, making an effort to learn basic German phrases can go a long way in showing respect for the local culture. Simple greetings like "Guten Tag" (Good day) and "Danke" (Thank you) are appreciated and can help you connect with locals.

2. **Respect Personal Space:** Germans value their personal space and tend to maintain a greater distance when interacting with others, especially strangers. Be mindful of this cultural norm and avoid standing too close or engaging in overly familiar gestures.

3. **Punctuality:** Germans place a high value on punctuality and expect others to be on time for appointments, meetings, and social gatherings. Arrive promptly or even a few minutes early to show respect for others' time and commitments.

4. **Appreciate the Food and Drink:** German cuisine is diverse and delicious, featuring hearty dishes like sausages, pretzels, and schnitzel, as well as world-renowned beers and wines. Embrace the local culinary traditions and savor the flavors of Germany's regional specialties.

5. **Follow Social Etiquette:** German social etiquette places emphasis on politeness, directness, and honesty. Be courteous when interacting with others, greet people with a firm handshake and maintain eye contact, and address them using their title and last name unless invited to use their first name.

6. **Respect the Environment:** Germans are committed to environmental conservation and sustainability. Follow recycling and waste management practices, minimize your carbon footprint, and respect natural habitats and wildlife when exploring outdoor areas.

7. **Cultural Events and Traditions:** Germany is home to a wealth of cultural events and traditions, from Oktoberfest celebrations to Christmas markets and folk festivals. Take the opportunity to participate in these cultural experiences with an open mind and respect for local customs.

8. **Educate Yourself:** Take the time to learn about Germany's history, art, literature, and music to gain a deeper appreciation for the country's cultural heritage.

Visit museums, galleries, and historical sites to enrich your understanding of German culture and its contributions to the world.

9. **Be Open-Minded:** Germany is a diverse and multicultural society, and travelers should approach cultural differences with an open mind and respect for diversity. Embrace the opportunity to learn from different perspectives and engage in meaningful cross-cultural exchanges.

By embracing German culture with respect and courtesy, travelers can forge meaningful connections, gain a deeper understanding of the country's traditions, and create lasting memories of their time in Germany. Approach each cultural experience with an open heart and a willingness to learn, and you'll be rewarded with enriching and memorable experiences.

APPENDIX

Useful Phrases & Expressions

Navigating Germany is made easier when travelers familiarize themselves with some essential phrases and expressions. Here are some useful ones to know:

1. **Greetings:**
   - "Guten Morgen" (Good morning)
   - "Guten Tag" (Good day)
   - "Guten Abend" (Good evening)
   - "Hallo" (Hello)
   - "Wie geht es Ihnen?" (How are you?)
   - "Auf Wiedersehen" (Goodbye)

2. **Politeness:**
   - "Bitte" (Please)
   - "Danke" (Thank you)
   - "Entschuldigung" (Excuse me/I'm sorry)
   - "Kein Problem" (No problem)
   - "Es tut mir leid" (I'm sorry)
   - "Bitte schön" (You're welcome)

3. **Basic Conversational Phrases:**
   - "Sprechen Sie Englisch?" (Do you speak English?)
   - "Ich verstehe nicht" (I don't understand)
   - "Können Sie das bitte wiederholen?" (Can you please repeat that?)

- "Wo ist die Toilette?" (Where is the bathroom?)
- "Wie viel kostet das?" (How much does it cost?)
- "Kann ich mit Kreditkarte zahlen?" (Can I pay with credit card?)

4. Ordering Food and Drinks:
- "Ich hätte gerne..." (I would like...)
- "Eine Tasse Kaffee, bitte" (A cup of coffee, please)
- "Ein Bier, bitte" (A beer, please)
- "Die Rechnung, bitte" (The check, please)
- "Guten Appetit" (Enjoy your meal)

5. Asking for Directions:
- "Entschuldigung, wo ist...?" (Excuse me, where is...?)
- "Können Sie mir helfen?" (Can you help me?)
- "Wie komme ich zum Bahnhof?" (How do I get to the train station?)
- "Ist es weit?" (Is it far?)
- "Links/rechts/geradeaus" (Left/right/straight ahead)

6. Emergency Phrases:
- "Hilfe!" (Help!)
- "Rufen Sie die Polizei!" (Call the police!)
- "Rufen Sie einen Arzt!" (Call a doctor!)
- "Wo ist das nächste Krankenhaus?" (Where is the nearest hospital?)
- "Feuer!" (Fire!)

7. Numbers:

- "Eins, zwei, drei, vier, fünf" (One, two, three, four, five)
- "Zehn, zwanzig, dreißig, vierzig, fünfzig" (Ten, twenty, thirty, forty, fifty) of
- "Hundert" (Hundred)
- "Tausend" (Thousand)

8. **Expressions of Gratitude:**
- "Vielen Dank" (Many thanks)
- "Danke schön" (Thank you very much)
- "Ich schätze das wirklich" (I really appreciate that)
- "Das ist sehr nett von Ihnen" (That's very kind of you)
- "Ich bin Ihnen sehr dankbar" (I am very grateful to you)

Learning and using these phrases and expressions will not only facilitate communication but also show respect for the local language and culture. Practice them before your trip and don't hesitate to use them when interacting with locals in Germany.

Additional Resources for Cultural Understanding

Enhancing your cultural understanding of Germany can enrich your travel experience and deepen your appreciation for the country's heritage. Here are some additional resources to aid in your cultural exploration:

1. **Books:**
   - "Germania: A Personal History of Germans Ancient and Modern" by Simon Winder
   - "The Germans" by Gordon A. Craig
   - "German Culture: Past and Present" by Ernest Belfort Bax

2. **Online Courses and Language Apps:**
   - Duolingo: Offers German language lessons for beginners to advanced learners.
   - Babbel: Provides interactive language courses focusing on practical conversation skills.
   - Goethe-Institut: Offers online courses in German language and culture.

3. **Cultural Events and Festivals:**
   - Oktoberfest: Experience Germany's famous beer festival held annually in Munich.
   - Christmas Markets: Visit traditional Christmas markets across Germany during the holiday season.
   - Carnival (Karneval): Participate in colorful parades and festivities celebrated in various regions of Germany.

4. **Museums and Cultural Institutions:**
   - Deutsches Historisches Museum (German Historical Museum) in Berlin: Offers insights into Germany's history and cultural heritage.
   - Museum Ludwig in Cologne: Features modern art collections and exhibitions.

- Neuschwanstein Castle in Bavaria: Explore one of Germany's most iconic landmarks and learn about its history.

5. **Local Cultural Experiences:**
  - Attend classical music concerts, opera performances, or theater productions in cities like Berlin, Munich, and Dresden.
  - Explore traditional villages, markets, and folklore events in rural areas to experience authentic German customs and traditions.

6. **Online Forums and Communities:**
  - Reddit: Join subreddits such as r/Germany or r/languagelearning to connect with fellow travelers, expatriates, and language enthusiasts for cultural insights and tips.
  - Expatriate Forums: Explore online forums and expatriate communities for firsthand experiences and advice from people living in Germany.

7. **Travel Guides and Blogs:**
  - Germany by The Rover: Offers comprehensive travel guides with cultural insights, detailed information on locations, maps, itineraries for family, couples & solo travelers, practical travel tips, food and so much more.
  - The Culture Trip: Features articles, guides, and travel recommendations highlighting German culture, cuisine, and attractions.

8. **Cultural Workshops and Courses:**

- Check local community centers, language schools, or cultural institutes for workshops, classes, or cultural exchange programs focused on German language, cuisine, music, or arts.

By utilizing these additional resources for cultural understanding, you'll gain deeper insights into Germany's rich cultural tapestry and foster a greater appreciation for its traditions, history, and people. Immerse yourself in the diverse cultural offerings of Germany and create memorable experiences that will last a lifetime.